I0162269

The Bible VS The Trinity

The Return of Adam

Apologetics

"It is better to listen to the rebuke of the wise, than to listen to the praise of fools"

King Solomon

Published by
COGITARE

Written By
Soeres Ramadhin

Foreword

Apologetics is defending the true message of God.
This writing provides a brief explanation of the Trinity compared to the identity of Jesus.
After explaining what the Trinity is, an arrangement of Biblical verses is presented that Trinitarians consider to be a foundation for the Trinity dogma.

The Bible is checked for the meaning of the verses, and a limited commentary is given.
All commentary is backed up with bible verses.

After this the identity of Jesus compared to Adam will be examined, followed by a consideration of whether it is possible that Jesus is the returned Adam.

Ephesians 5:11

And have no fellowship with the unfruitful works of darkness, <u>but rather reprove them</u>.

1 Peter 3:15

But sanctify the Lord God in your hearts<u>, and be ready always to give an answer</u> to every man who asketh you a reason for the hope that is in you, with meekness and fear.

Content

Bible verses used by Trinitarians

What is the Bible

The term bible comes from the Koine Greek language and means **'collection of many books'**. Throughout history, religious Hebrew books written by different authors were gathered and bundled together by people. Such a bundle of books is termed a 'biblia', or a 'bible'. These books have stored the sayings and actions of God and of those who worked for or against Him.

The Bible has two parts: the Old Covenant (this part describes primarily the history and progress of the covenant made by God and the Hebrews) and the New Covenant (this part describes the covenant made by God and all the nations). The Old Covenant scriptures were written in a period in which people spoke Hebrew and Aramaic. The New Covenant scriptures were written in a period in which people spoke also Koine Greek.

Different bibles (Catholic & Protestant)

Due to unknown authorship or to other uncertainties, a small number of books are termed **apocryphal**, meaning that they cannot be proven to be authentic. The necessary conditions for a book to be termed authentic are that it is written in the time of its suggested author and that its message is in accordance with the other authentic books. The apocryphal books were reason for a large group of Christians (the Protestants) to protest and subsequently exclude these books from their Bible. However, the Catholic Church kept the apocryphal books in their Bible, and thus two Bible books became available.

In the Bible the word of God can be found, but the Bible as a whole isn't the word of God.

Those who claim that the Bible itself is the word of God are actually saying that God had more to say to the Catholics with their 73 books than to the protestants with 66 books.

The Catholic Church has bundled together 73 books.
The Protestant Church has bundled together 66 books, excluding
7 books named:

1. Tobit.
2. Judith.
3. 1 Maccabees.
4. 2 Maccabees.
5. Wisdom of Solomon.
6. Wisdom of Sirach (also called Ecclesiasticus)
7. Baruch including the Letter of Jeremiah.

*parts of the books of Esther and Daniel

Nonetheless, the authentic books (such as the Gospels) appear in both
the Catholic and Protestant Bibles.
Next to the prophetic books are the letters (epistles) of the disciples,
who provided their understanding of the prophecies and
commandments given by Jesus or God.

Translation errors

Sending the divine message to humans is God's work and is without
error; however, writing, translating, and copying the divine message
into Aramaic, Hebrew, English, Arabic, or other languages is human
work and will contain human errors. When God ordered Moses to
write the Law and give copies to each of the twelve tribes of Israel,
He knew that with time human copying-errors could occur. For this
reason, He ordered that the original manuscript of the Law be kept in
the tabernacle, as a witness against false teachings.
Deuteronomy 31:26
Take this book of the law, and put it in the side of the Ark of the
Covenant of the LORD your God, *that it may be there for a witness
against thee.*

Such errors or fabrications are possible with every copied piece of writing, including the copies of the biblical books.
God is aware of this and gave a fair warning to those who intentionally distort His message.
According to God, it is possible to distort the message in the Bible, but not without consequences.
Revelation 22:19
And if any man shall *take away from the words of the book* of this prophecy, God shall take away his part out of the book of life, and out of the holy city, and from the things which are written in this book.

Deuteronomy 4:2
You shall not add **to the word which I command you,** *nor take from it,* that you may keep the commandments of the Lord your God which I command you.

From 1898 unto 2012 the Nestle-Aland (NA) Novum Testamentum Graece developed by Eberhard Nestle, Kurt Aland, Bruce Metzger and Carlo Martini.
The Bible versions based on their editions are for example: The New English Translation (NET), the New International Version (NIV), Nieuw Bijbel Genootschap (NBG).

These versions removed many verses and words, this is why the NA editions has been rejected by many Bible reading Christians respecting the warning given in the Bible:
Revelation 22:19
And if any man shall take away from the words of the book of this prophecy, God shall take away his part out of the book of life...

Comparing the NA editions with the KJV:

1. In Acts 8:37 the criteria for being baptized is removed by the NET translators:

    NET- Empty

KJV
And Philip said, If thou believest with all thine heart, thou mayest. And he answered and said, *I believe that Jesus Christ is the Son of God.*

2. In the NIV Luke 2:33 questions the virgin birth by describing Joseph as the father of Jesus:

NIV
The *child's father* and mother marveled at what was said about him

KJV
And *Joseph* and his mother marveled at those things which were spoken of him

3. In the NET translation, Deuteronomy 22:28 reads that a raped woman must marry her rapist:

NET
Suppose a man comes across a virgin who is not engaged and overpowers and *rapes* her and they are discovered. The man who has raped her must pay her father fifty shekels of silver **and *she must become his wife*** because he has violated her; he may never divorce her as long as he lives.

KJV
If a man find a damsel that is a virgin, which is not betrothed, and lay hold on her, and *lie with her*, and they be found;
Then the man that lay with her shall give unto the damsel's father fifty shekels of silver, ***and she shall be his wife***; because he hath humbled her, he may not put her away all his days.

4. In the NET translation, Isaiah 7:14 the miraculous sign of a virgin birth has been replaced by the sign of a normal birth:

NET
For this reason the sovereign master himself will give you a confirming sign. Look, *this young woman* is about to conceive and will give birth to a son. You, young woman, will name him Immanuel.

KJV
Therefore the Lord himself shall give you a sign; Behold, *a virgin shall conceive,* and bear a son, and shall call his name Immanuel.

One of the Gospel writers quoted Isaiah, whereby we know what the correct translation should be.

NET
Matthew 1:23
"Look! *The virgin* **will conceive** and give birth to a son, and they will name him Emmanuel," which means "God with us."

As I said before sending the divine message to humans is God's work and is without error; however, writing, translating, and copying the divine message is human work and will contain human errors.
Our sole concern is to be alert for significant translation errors, which are easily discovered when the context of a verse has become illogical or distorted or when it contradicts the other books.

The following are examples of translation errors that have been corrected in the KJV:

King James translation in 1944:
"Owl" instead of "own"
1 Peter 3:5 "For after this manner in the old time the holy women also, who trusted God, adorned themselves, being in subjection to their _owl_ husbands."

King James translation in 1823:
"Camels" instead of "damsels"
Genesis 24:61 "And Rebecca arose, **and her** _camels,_ and they rode upon the camels, and followed the man: and the servant took Rebecca and went his way."

For centuries Christians read Bible versions such as the King James or De Statenvertaling which are based on the Textus Receptus (a Greek translation of the New Testament written by Erasmus in 1516) and the Masoretic Text (the Hebrew text of the Old Testament).

Thanks to the discovery of the Dead Sea Scrolls (ancient biblical manuscripts) in 1947, we see that the main message of the Dead Sea Scrolls is almost identical to the modern translation of the KJV Bible we have today.

We can therefore conclude that the main message of the versions based on the Textus Receptus remains close to God's original message.

How to read and understand the Bible

The Bible is capable of explaining its own verses.
This is the best approach for understanding scripture, as the prophet Isaiah said:

Isaiah 28:10
For precept must be upon precept, precept upon precept; *line upon line, line upon line; here a little, and there a little.*

Context is very important

Moreover, each word in the Bible must be read within its full context. This is very important to prevent distortions or hasty assumptions:

2 Peter 3:16
He speaks about this subject in all his letters. **Some things in them are hard to understand,** *which ignorant and unstable people distort, leading to their own destruction, as they* **do the rest of the Scriptures.**

For example, in the following sentence, the context determines the meaning of the word 'date':

1. Grandmother's favorite fruit to eat is a date (fruit).
2. I took the woman out on a date (social activity).

By taking the other words (the context) into consideration, the meaning of the word 'date' becomes clear.

Its also very important to distinguish between the sayings and action of men and the sayings and actions of God.

For example:
If the text states that a king or prophet approves of polygamy or idolatry.
than this should be treated as the opinion and action of only that person, for example:
Prophet Elijah said:
1 king 19:4
..and he(Elijah) requested for himself that he might die, and said, "It is enough; now, O LORD, take my life, for I am not better than my fathers.

but when the text reads the prophet said:
Thus said the Lord….. then we can consider it as a saying from God.

Origin of the Trinity

The Trinity of gods was an ancient doctrine that came from ancient Asia called the Tri-murti that consists of:

1.Brahma the creator
2. Vishnu the preserver
3. Shiva the destroyer

This concept developed and spread over the other pagan cultures including the Romans.
The Roman Trinity of Diana consist of the idols:

1. Phoebe
2. Diana
3. Proserpina.

During the rise of Christianity, these Roman dogmas were on the verge of collapse. If the pagan leaders wanted to maintain the doctrine respecting the trinity of their gods, it was necessary for them to compromise with the growing Christian community.
Acts 19:27
So that not only this our craft is in danger to be set at nought; but also that the temple of the great goddess **Diana** should be despised, and her magnificence should be destroyed, *whom all Asia and the world worshippeth.*

Therefore, in the year 325 A.D., Roman Emperor Constantine the Great convened a gathering called the Council of Nicea. During this council, the Trinity dogma was accepted by some church leaders which then gained authority; this was the beginning of the Roman church persecuting the other not cooperating churches.
Today there are many mega-churches that still follow the Trinity and they are very entrenched respecting this dogma.

Trinitarians also claim that God consists of three persons: God the Son, God the Father, and God the Holy Spirit. These three persons form one being, or as they describe Him, a Triune God.

Trinitarian teacher James White about the Trinity:

Quote:
"Within the **one Being** that is God, there exists eternally **three coequal** and coeternal **persons**, namely, the Father, the Son, and the Holy Spirit." (The Forgotten Trinity)

(James White doesnt realize that the three persons are also beings.)

The Catholic church:

Quote:
"The Trinity is a **mystery** of faith in the strict sense, one of the "mysteries that are hidden in God, which can never be known unless they are revealed by God". (Catechism of the Catholic Church 2:237)

What type of being is God: spiritual or organical?

Trinitarian teacher James White **differentiate between beings and persons**. He claims that there is one being with three persons.

Quote:
"Note immediately that we are not saying there are three Beings that are one Being, or three persons that are one person. Such would be self-contradictory. I emphasize this because, most often, this is the misrepresentation of the doctrine that is commonly found in the literature of various religions that deny the Trinity."

(The forgotten Trinity, pg. 27)

J White doesn't realize that a being is defined as something or someone that lives.

There are two types of beings:

1. Spiritual beings (persons)
2. Organical beings (trees, bacteria, our body, etc.)

The Bible clearly describes that God is a person and therefore a spiritual being.
John 4:24
God is a Spirit: and they that worship him must worship him in spirit and in truth.

Regarding God's being, the teachings of the Trinitarian Churches are unclear. Trinitarians agree that three persons cannot be one person and therefore claim that God is a being that consists of three persons. As the three persons of which He consists are also beings, the ensuing question is what type of being He is. That God is not a person implies that He is an organic being that houses three different spiritual beings, which are treated as three separate gods living in one being. In Mark 16:9, there is an example that is coherent with this view, in which a human body (the organic being) consist of multiple persons (spiritual beings).

Common explanations:

1. A human being also consists of three parts: mind, body, and soul.
2. A family also consists of three parts: mother, father, and children.

From this perspective, they explain that God consists of three persons: Father, Son, and Holy Spirit. The problem with both examples is that they do not explain how three persons are equally the same.

Example of the human

It is true that a human being consists of mind, body, and soul, but these three parts are not coequal.

Also from these three parts, only the soul is the person. The body is the house in which the soul resides, and the mind is the term for the activities that it performs, such as thought, perception, emotions, will, memories, and imagination. The organic human being (the body) consists only of one spiritual being.

Example of the family

The example of the family is equally inapplicable to the Trinity. Mother, father, and children are indeed multiple persons who together form one family. However, a family is not a being or a person, but rather a social unit of closely related persons, whereas God is a living being rather than a social unit.

The early churches

Trinitarian churches are in a great majority, should this be a reason to accept the Trinity?
According to prophecy many different false churches will arise.
And they will do many marvelous works in his name.

Matthew 7:22
Many will say to me in that day, Lord, Lord, have we not prophesied *in thy name? and in thy name have cast out devils? and in thy name done many wonderful works?* And then will I profess unto them, **I never knew you: depart from me,** *ye that work iniquity.*

Matthew 24:24
For there shall arise **false Christs**, and false prophets, *and shall shew great signs and wonders*; insomuch that, if it were possible, they shall deceive the very elect.

Sources of early church fathers, outside of the biblical sources.
Consider that only two of the seven churches were loyal and sincere during the time of the early Christians.

More than half of the early churches were following a false gospel.

Early Churches keeping the Gospel:

- Smyrna (Revelation 2:8-11) – The church admired for its tribulation and poverty; forecast to suffer persecution (2:10)

- Philadelphia (Revelation 3:7-13) – The church steadfast in faith, that had kept God's word and endured patiently (3:10)

Early Churches that were led astray:

- **Ephesus** (Revelation 2:1-7) rebuked for having forsaken its first love (2:4)

- **Pergamos** (Revelation 2:12-17) -- The church with false teachers and where 'Satan's seat' or 'throne' is (2:16)

- **Thyatira** (Revelation 2:18-29) held the teachings of a false prophetess (2:20)

- **Sardis** (Revelation 3:1-6) -- The church whose faith was inactive or death(3:2-3)

- **Laodicea**, (Revelation 3:14-22) -- The church that was lukewarm (3:16)

Early Church fathers

Trinitarians use quotes from early bishops, such as Ignatius of Antioch. Trinitarians consider them as their earliest church father, but according to Jesus, the Christians have only one church Father and one Teacher.

Matthew 23:9
And do not call anyone on earth 'father,' for you have one Father, and he is in heaven. Nor are you to be called teacher, for you have one teacher, the Christ.

Documents of early Christians such as Irenaeus, Athanasius and Eusebius should be read with cautiousness and tested if they are in line with the Gospel.

Paul saw the spread of a false and confusing Gospel.
Galatians 1:6
I am astonished that you are so soon removed from the one who called you to live in the grace of Christ and are turning to *another gospel which is really no gospel at all*. **But some people cause confusion** and are trying to pervert the gospel of Christ. But though we, or an angel from heaven, preach any other gospel unto you than that which we have preached unto you, let him be accursed. As we said before, so say I now again, *if any man preach any other gospel unto you than that ye have received, let him be accursed..*

The apostles mentioned the early rise of false teachers.

2 Corinthians 11:13
For such are false apostles, deceitful workers, transforming themselves into the apostles of Christ.
And no marvel; for Satan himself is transformed into an angel of light.
Therefore it is no great thing if his ministers also be transformed as the ministers of righteousness; whose end shall be according to their works.

Miracles should also be treated with caution, because the Antichrist can perform misleading miracles.

Revelation 13:14
And deceiveth them that dwell on the earth by the means of those miracles which he had power to do in the sight of the beast;

Bible verses used by Trinitarians

Argument 1

John 8:58
Before Abraham was, *I am.*

Does this verse mean that Jesus is God?
Trinitarians believe that the name of God was revealed as "I AM" and that Jesus referred to this in John 8:58.

Exodus 3:14
And God said to Moses, YHWH ("I AM who I AM.")And He said, "Thus you shall say to the children of Israel, *"I AM has sent me to you."*

Most Trinitarians entirely ignore the following verse, in which God declares His name:
Exodus 3:15
Tell them... **the Lord God of your fathers, the God of Abraham, the God of Isaac, and the God of Jacob**, hath sent me unto you: **this is my name for ever**, and this is my memorial unto all generations.

In order to understand why God said, "I AM has sent me to you", it is useful to look at the context of Exodus 3. When God told Moses to go to the Israelites, Moses asked for His name.
Exodus 3:13
And Moses said unto God, Behold, when I come unto the children of Israel, and shall say unto them, *The God of your fathers* hath sent me unto you; and they shall say to me, *What is His name*? What shall I say unto them?

God does not have parents or creators who named Him and He already told Moses who He was in verse 6.
Exodus 3:6

Moreover **He said, I am the God of thy father, the God of Abraham, the God of Isaac, and the God of Jacob**. And Moses hid his face; for he was afraid to look upon God.

After God made Himself known to Moses, Moses still asked for His name. God's response to Moses was therefore, **"I am that I am"** or **"I shall be that I shall be"**.

Because God always introduced Himself to the forefathers of the Israelites as **"I AM** the Lord God", **"I AM** the God of Bethel", **"I AM** God Almighty", and so forth, He then said to Moses,
"Tell them **I AM** has sent you".
The most probable reason for God to say to Moses, "tell them I AM has sent you", is to ensure that people would recognize that the God of their forefathers was being introduced.

In the following verse God established His name for all generations:
Exodus 3:15
Tell them...*The Lord God* of your fathers, the God of Abraham, the God of Isaac, and the God of Jacob, hath sent me unto you: *this is my name for ever, and this is my memorial unto all generations.*

Within the context of Exodus 3, the name of God is neither "I AM" nor "Jesus", but rather "the Lord (YHWH) God of Abraham", "the God of Isaac", and "the God of Jacob".

Having established the name of God, the question remains whether Jesus referred to himself as being the "I AM" from Exodus 3.

Jesus said:
Before Abraham was, I am.
The original Koine Greek for "I AM" in this verse is "Ego Eimi", meaning, "I exist". Consequently, the verse from John should be understood as: "before Abraham was, **I exist**".

Contextual meaning: Jesus existed before Abraham existed.

The false explanation: Jesus said: before Abraham was, my name is I AM.
 Beside Jesus, many others in the Bible used the words "I am ". For example:
1 Kings 18:7-8
Now as Obadiah was on his way, suddenly Elijah met him; and he recognized him, and fell on his face, and said, "Is that you, my lord Elijah?"
And he answered him, *"I am.* Go, tell thy lord, 'Elijah is here.'"

When Obadiah fell on his face and asked Elijah if he is lord, Elijah responded: "I am". According to Trinitarian logic, the fact that Elijah replied with "I am" should mean that Elijah is God.
According to Biblical logic, Elijah simply confirmed that he was an earthly lord.

A second example is that of the people asking John who he is:
John 1:22-23
What do you say about yourself? He said: "**I am (Ego Eimi)**..."

In these examples, it is clear that when people use the words "I am", they are not necessarily referring to Gods usage of I AM in Exodus 3:14.

Since Jesus received glory from the God of Abraham, Isaac and Jacob and therefore cannot be the God of Abraham, Isaac and Jacob.

Acts 3:13
The **God of Abraham, and of Isaac, and of Jacob,** the God of our fathers**, hath glorified his Son Jesus**; whom ye delivered up, and denied him in the presence of Pilate, when he was determined to let him go.

Conclusion

Jesus claimed to exist before Abraham.
Elijah claimed to be lord over Obadiah.
John claimed to be the one who was prophesied by Isaiah. Placed within context, it becomes clear that none of them claimed to be the "I AM" or Ego Eimi from Exodus 3:14.

In John 8:58 it is only possible to know what "I AM " means after determining what the phrase "before Abraham WAS" means. The words "was" and "am" in John 8:58 refers to being born, not being God.

Argument 2

Matthew 9:28
And when he was come into the house, the blind men came to him:
and Jesus saith unto them, Believe ye that I am able to do this? They
said unto him, *Yea, **Lord.***

Does the fact that Jesus was called "Lord" mean that he is God? The
term "Lord" is not equivalent to "God". In the Bible many kings,
prophets and even angels are called "lord".
A heavenly lord.

Zechariah 6:4
Then I answered and said unto the angel that talked with me, What
are these, *my **lord?***

An earthly lord.

1 Kings 18:7-8
Now as Obadiah was on his way, suddenly Elijah met him; and he
recognized him, and fell on his face, and said, "Is that you, ***my lord***
Elijah?"

Conclusion
Within the Biblical context, it becomes clear that Obadiah is not
referring to Elijah as the Lord God, and that he falls on his face
merely out of respect for the prophet, rather than in a state of religious
worship. In the New Testament (N.T.) this type of behavior has not
changed: when people met Jesus they called him "lord" and fell on
their faces, just as Obadiah did when he met Elijah.

These verses show that Elijah the prophet and the angel were also
lords, but they were addressed as one of the many earthly and
heavenly lords.

This refutes the argument that Jesus is God because he was called "lord".

The King (Messiah) is also addressed as "lord".
But God is Lord over lords, including the Messiah, prophets, and angels.
Deuteronomy 10:17
For the LORD your God is *God of gods*, and Lord of lords.

Argument 3

Matt 1:23
Behold, the virgin shall be with child, and bear a Son, and they shall call his name Immanuel, which is translated, "**God with us**."

Jesus is Immanu-EL.
There are two viewpoints regarding the meaning of "Immanuel":
1. Jesus is literally God with us (the Trinitarian viewpoint).
2. Jesus is **the sign** that God is with us.

To decide which viewpoint is Biblical, it is necessary to consult the Bible to understand what the name means.

In the Bible there are numerous names that begin or end with EL (God).

Some examples include:
- EL-yashiyb
- Micha-EL
- Isra-EL
- EL-jakim
- Gabri-EL.

The prophet Samuel's name, for instance, means: "God has heard".
Using the Trinitarian method, we could claim that the prophet is literally God who heard.
In the Biblical method, this means that the birth of the prophet is the sign that God has heard.

Another prophet who received the name "John/Yehohanan" meaning "God is gracious".
Using the trinitarian method we could say that John is God who is gracious, but the biblical method is that John is the sign of God's grace.

John lived up to this name by washing away the sins of many. Throughout the Bible God gave people such as Abram, Jacob, Sarai, and even the messiah a new name with a new meaning, according to the sign that they would become in the future.

For example:

- Abram's new name:
  Genesis 17:5
  No longer shall your name be called Abram, but your name shall <u>be Abraham</u>; for I have made you a father of many nations.

- Jacob's new name:
  Genesis 35:10
  And God said to him, "Your name is Jacob; your name shall not be called Jacob anymore, <u>but Israel</u> shall be your name." So He called his name Israel.

- Jesus' new name:
  Revelation 3: 12
  He who overcomes, I will make him a pillar in the temple of My God, and he shall go out no more. I will write on him the name of My God and the name of the city of My God, the New Jerusalem, which comes down out of heaven from My God. And I will write on him **my new name**.

Conclusion

The coming of Samuel is the sign that God has heard.
The coming of Immanuel is the sign that God is with us. From a Biblical perspective, neither Samuel nor Immanuel were literal God in person.

Argument 4

Jesus would be called "Mighty God". Does this mean that Jesus is our
God?

In Isaiah 9 it is predicted that "his name shall be called Wonderful,
Counselor, The mighty God, The everlasting Father, The prince of
Peace".
God gave an honest prediction stating that when this child will be
born *people* will call him different titles such as "mighty God", or
"prince of Peace". The prophecy that Jesus would be considered a
mighty God was fulfilled by doubting Thomas.

Conclusion

Trinitarians partly fulfilled this prophecy, but as Christians, one
should consider what God Himself called this child:

Argument 5

Mark 5:6-7
When he saw Jesus from afar, he ran and **worshiped him**. And he cried out with a loud voice and said, "What have I to do with You, Jesus, Son of the Most High God? I implore You by God that You do not torment me."

Does the fact that Jesus was worshipped mean that he is a god?

To consider this, it must be determined whether Jesus and his followers are worshipped as gods.
Jesus said to the Christians:

Revelation 3:9
I will make them to come and **worship** before thy feet, and to know that I have loved thee.

If one uses the Trinitarian method, then one could also claim that Christians will be worshiped and are therefore God, which would entail that there is no trinity, but rather a millionity.

Context is of great importance, for instance when reading in the Old Testament (O.T.) that Abraham prayed to his servant:
Genesis 24:2
And Abraham said unto his eldest servant of his house, that ruled over all that he had,
Put, *I pray thee*, thy hand under my thigh.

Since Abraham prayed towards his servant Trinitarians could claim that the servant of Abraham is God, but the Bible has certain commandments, and these should always be taught within their full context. For example:
Exodus 20:4
Thou shalt not make unto thee any graven image...

For example Moses made a graven image of a serpent:
Numbers 21:9
So **Moses made a bronze serpent**, and put it on a pole; and so it was,
if a serpent had bitten anyone, when he looked at the bronze serpent...

But the commandment forbade graven images:
Exodus 20:4
Thou shalt not make unto thee any graven image, or any likeness
of any thing that is in heaven above, or that is in the earth beneath, or
that is in the water under the earth.

This does not mean that Moses disobeyed the commandment given in
Exodus 20:4.
The contextual meaning of the commandment is to not create any
graven image to be a god.
The bronze serpent was not created to be a god. The same is true for
worship.

Do not worship anyone or anything else to be your god.
Exodus 34:14
For thou shalt **worship no other god**: for the Lord, whose name is
Jealous, is a jealous God:

But did Jesus receive religious worship?

The disciples saw how people showed reverence to Jesus. The gesture of showing reverence to the Messiah/King was translated and written in Koine Greek as "proskuneo".
For Trinitarians, the confusion begins with this word, because proskuneo is a homonym: a word that is used for multiple behaviors.

Thayer's Greek Lexicon offers the following definition:

1. To kiss the hand to (towards) one, in token of reverence.
2. Among the Orientals, especially the Persians, to fall upon the knees and touch the ground with the forehead as an expression of profound reverence.
3. **In the N.T. by kneeling or prostration to do homage**
The Greek writers used "proskuneo" for two different actions:
1. Reverence towards the Jewish high priest.
2. **Worship towards God.**

To understand what type of proskuneo (reverence or worship) was given to Jesus, the book of Revelation should be consulted.
Revelation 3:9
Behold, I will make them of the synagogue of Satan, which say they are Jews, and are not, but do lie; behold, I will make them to come and **worship (proskuneo)** before thy feet, and to know that I have loved thee.

Proskuneo here means showing reverence before their feet, and Jesus received the same type of proskuneo.
Jesus was given reverence as the son of God.
Matt 14:33
....and **worshiped him, saying, "*Truly you are the son of God*"**

The loyal Christians will also be given reverence not as God, but as those who are loved by Jesus.

Conclusion

The Koine Greek word "proskuneo" has multiple meanings. In order to decide between reverence and worship, one must take into consideration the context of the verses. In the case of Jesus and the Christians, they were not worshiped or prayed to as being God, but rather received reverence as being the son of God, and as Jesus' loved ones.

Argument 6

John 10:30
I and My Father are one.

Does the verse "Jesus and God are one" imply that Jesus is God?
Jesus explains what being one with God means:
John 17:11
...that **they may be one just as we are**

This verse shows that Christians must be one with each other just as God and Jesus are one. This clearly indicates towards being one in unity rather than to be one being. For example, Peter and Matthew are not one in being, but one in unity. Jesus and God are therefore also one in unity, as Peter and Matthew are one in unity.
Further examples of one in unity include:
Genesis 11:6
...Behold, **the people is one**, and they have all one language

John 17:21

That they all may be one, as You, Father, are in Me, and I in You; that they also may be one in Us, that the world may believe that You sent Me. And the **glory which You gave Me I have given them**, that they may be one just as We are one.

.

From these verses we see that God is in Jesus as Jesus is in his followers. This does not mean that Peter and others transformed into Jesus, because Jesus is said to be in them as God is also in him. Rather, it indicates that the teachings, words and works of Jesus are in them as the teachings, words and works of God are in Jesus.

Conclusion
Jesus and the Father are one in unity and not one in person or being.

Argument 7

John 14:9
...He who has seen me has seen the Father...

Does this mean that Jesus IS the Father?
The invisible God created a living image of Himself. If one has seen this image one has seen God.

John 12:44
Jesus cried and said, He that believeth on me, *believeth not on me, but on him that sent me.* 45 And *he that seeth me seeth Him that sent me.*

Adam is the image of God.
Genesis 5:1
This is the book of the generations of Adam. In the day that God created man, in the likeness of God **made he him** (singular).

Jesus is the image of God.
2 Corinthians 4:4
..lest the light of the glorious gospel of Christ, who **is the image of God**, should shine unto them.

Conclusion

When one sees Jesus/Adam, one has seen the image of the Father. However, this does not entail that Jesus/Adam is God. For example Seth is the direct image of Adam, but is not Adam in person.

Genesis 5:3

And Adam lived an hundred and thirty years, and **begat a son** in his own likeness, and **after his image**; and called his name Seth.

Likewise, the son of God is the direct image of God, but is not God himself. If one has seen the mercy, love, righteousness, and wisdom of Jesus, one has seen the spiritual image of God.

Argument 8

John 1:1
In the beginning was the word, and the word was with God, *and the word was God.*

Does the word always refer to Jesus?
In view of the fact that Jesus is titled as The Word of God,
Trinitarians assume that 'The word" in John 1:1 stands for the person
Jesus, so in their mind they read: In the beginning was Jesus, and
Jesus was with God, and Jesus was God.

However, the Bible differentiate between the word as the title of a
person and the word that is the spoken breath of God.
So we should consult the Bible if the word in the beginning was a
spoken word or a person.
Psalm 33:6
By **the word of the Lord** were the heavens made; and all the host of
them by the **breath of his mouth**.
He gathereth the waters of the sea together as an heap: he layeth up
the depth in storehouses.
Let all the earth fear the Lord: let all the inhabitants of the world
stand in awe of him.
For **he spake**, and it was done; he commanded, and it stood fast.

Psalm 33 explains that the word in the beginning was a spoken word.
The Gospel according to John begins with a reference to the account
in Genesis.
According to Genesis 1 it is indeed stated that there was only God and
His word, and with nothing but His words He started to create the
heavens and the Earth.
John 1:1 offers a description of how God and His spoken words are
one and of how God created everything with His words.
Genesis 1:3
...and God *said* (the words) let there be...

The Word that became flesh;
On the sixth day God created a spiritual being in God's own image
and so God blew His holy Spirit into the flesh of man."

Genesis 2:7
And the Lord God formed man of the dust of the ground, and
breathed into his nostrils the breath of life; and man became a
living soul.

Job 27:3
All the while my breath is in me, and *the spirit of God is in my
nostrils.*

This image of God lived with God and "all things" were made
through him and in him was the life to give to his offspring.
John 1:2
He was in the beginning with God. **All things were made through
him**, and without him nothing was made that was made. In him was
life, **and the life was the light of men.**

However, the phrase "all things were made through him" does not
imply that through Jesus literally all things, such as the sun, the moon
and the sea-creatures were created. "All things" could also refer to all
human life. Through Adam's flesh and bones the woman was created,
and from them all humans were created, for he is the first created and
we are created by him and for him, as his offspring.

"All things" and "all creation" sometimes means all humans.
Mark 16:15
And He said to them, "Go into all the world and preach the gospel to
every *creature*

Genesis 3:20

And Adam called his wife's name Eve, because she was <u>the mother of</u> <u>*all living*</u>.

Colossians 1:15
He is **the image** of **the invisible** God, the **firstborn** over **all creation**.

It should be clear that in Colossians, Mark and Genesis, "every creature", "all creation" and "all living" refer to all human life, rather than to the moon, the trees, the insects, etc.

Conclusion

The spoken words are God's way to create matter.
The Bible explains that the Son of God is that word that turned into flesh, and that when the spirit of God was breathed into the nostrils of Adams flesh it contained a living soul, and so His Son was begotten.

Jesus is only that word that became flesh, and this occurred in Genesis. This means that one can not randomly select where one wants "the word" to be the equivalent of Jesus Christ or to be a spoken sentence. If Trinitarians wish to argue that "the word" always refers to Jesus Christ , they will encounter a problem of inconsistency with the appearance of "the word" in other parts, such as Deuteronomy.
Deuteronomy 4:2
You shall not add to *the word* which I command you, nor take from it, that you may keep the commandments of the Lord your God which I command you.

Argument 9

John 20:28
<u>Thomas answered and said</u> to Jesus "my lord and ***my God.***"

Does Thomas' answer make Jesus a god, and why did Jesus not stop him? Again, the Bible should be consulted.
Isaiah prophesied that Jesus would be called a mighty god and Thomas fulfilled this prophecy.

Isaiah 9:6
...And His name **will be called**
Wonderful, Counselor, Mighty God...

Jesus knew of this prophecy and did not attempt to stop Thomas from fulfilling it. Likewise, it was prophesied that Jesus would be betrayed by a friend, and he did not attempt to stop Judas or persuade him not to betray him. Jesus knew that he would be delivered and killed, and did not attempt to stop or flee from his accusers.
Other prophesies in the O.T. that Jesus did not stop include:

The betrayal by his friend
Psalm 41:9
Even my own familiar friend in whom I trusted,
Who ate my bread,
Has lifted up his heel against me.

His early death and suffering
Psalm 22:16
For dogs have surrounded Me;
The congregation of the wicked has enclosed Me.
They pierced My hands and My feet.

Isaiah 53:9
And he made His grave with the wicked, and with the rich at his
death, Because He had done no violence, nor was any deceit in his
mouth.

Jesus never attempted to stop prophecy and even referred to Peter as a
Satan, because Peter wanted to impede the prophecy by preventing
Jesus' capture.
Matthew 16:23
But he turned, and said unto Peter, Get thee behind me, Satan: thou
art an offence unto me: for thou are not mindful of the things that be
of God, but those that be of men.

Though he was frequently with Jesus, Thomas did not realize who
Jesus was. Thomas was an unbeliever who, despite seeing the
miracles of Jesus, and even after walking with Jesus and hearing him
say, 'I shall die, but after three days I shall rise again', considered this
impossible.
Matthew 16:21
From that time forth began Jesus to shew unto his disciples, how that
he must go unto Jerusalem, and suffer many things of the elders and
chief priests and scribes, and be killed, **and be raised again the third
day.**

The unbelieving Thomas said that it was impossible for Jesus to rise
from the dead.
John 20:25
But he (**Thomas**) said unto them, Except I shall see in his
hands the print of the nails, and put my finger into the print
of the nails, and thrust my hand into his side **I will not
believe.**

Jesus' response to doubting Thomas:
John 20:29
Jesus saith unto him, Thomas, because thou hast seen me, thou hast
believed: **blessed are they** that have not seen, and yet have believed.

Not in the least was Thomas blessed for his answer. For unbelievers like Thomas, witnessing such a miracle leads them to consider Jesus and other prophets to be a mighty god.

John 10:34

Jesus answered them, Is it not written in your law, **I said, Ye are gods?** *If he called them gods, unto whom the word of God came,*

The prophet Moses, for instance, was sent as a 'mighty' god towards the unbeliever Pharaoh.

Exodus 7:1

And the Lord said unto Moses, See, I have made **thee** *a god to Pharaoh*: and Aaron thy brother shall be thy prophet.

The prophet Daniel received worship and offerings from the unbeliever King Nebuchadnezzar:

Daniel 2:48

Then the **king Nebuchadnezzar** fell upon his face, and *worshipped Daniel*, and commanded that they should **offer an oblation and sweet odours unto him.**

These verses show that unbelievers saw or treated the prophets and the Messiah as mighty gods. Those who believe in the power of the unseen God, however, know that Moses, Daniel, and Jesus were prophets sent by God, and that their miracles came from God.

Conclusion

Through the unbelieving Thomas, the prophecy stating that Jesus would be called a mighty god was fulfilled. Some choose to trust the words of Thomas about Jesus; others choose to trust and follow the words of Jesus, John the prophet, and God Himself.

God says of Jesus:
Matt 3:17
This is *My beloved son*, with whom I am well pleased.

The prophet John says about Jesus:
John 1:34
I have seen and testified that this is **the Son of God.**

Jesus about himself:
John 10:36
...I said, "**I am the Son of God**"...

Argument 10

1 Tim 3:16

...God was **manifest in the flesh**...

Trinitarians claim that this verse shows that God was born as a man. Before consulting the Bible to explain this verse, it is important to note that it comes from Paul the evangelist. As this letter did not come from Jesus or a prophet, it is not fundamental in following Jesus Christ.

Many Jews who heard the Gospel of Jesus were saved before Paul wrote these letters, meaning that hearing the Gospel is sufficient for people to become Christians.

The apostle Peter also warned that Paul's letters are difficult for those who are too unstable to understand them, and that they result in distorting his letters.

2 Peter 3:16

And account that the longsuffering of our Lord is salvation; even as our beloved *brother Paul also according to the wisdom given unto him hath written unto you;*

As also in all his epistles, speaking in them of these things; *in which are some things hard to be understood,* which they that are unlearned and unstable wrest, as they do also the other scriptures, unto their own destruction.

In order to read Paul's letters correctly, it is important to follow his words closely. By doing so, one can understand what he meant by the manifestation of God's Spirit in the flesh, and place events in the correct order:

1. The prophecy appears in the O.T.

2. Jesus announces this prophecy in the N.T.

3. Paul witnessed the fulfilling of the prophecy.

1. The prophecy appears in the O.T.:
Joel 2:28-29
And it shall come to pass afterward, *that **I will pour out My Spirit upon all flesh**...*

2. Jesus announces the prophecy in the N.T.:
Matt 10:20
For it will not be you speaking, but the **Spirit of your Father speaking through you.**

3. The fulfilling of the Prophecy begins:
Acts 2:4
And they were *all filled with the Holy Spirit*, and began to speak with other tongues...

After Paul saw how the disciples where taken over by God's Holy Spirit he could only describe this as the manifestation of God's Spirit in our flesh.
1 Corinthians 12:7
But the *manifestation of the Spirit* is given *to every man* to profit withal.

The manifestation of God's Holy Spirit is as follows:
The body is a house or temple wherein one dwells. God's Holy Spirit can dwell simultaneously with one in one's body. The manifestation of God's Holy Spirit appears in Acts 2:4. This does not entail that the apostles transformed into God, for the spirit of Peter and the Spirit of God can dwell simultaneously in the body (temple) of the apostle Peter. Likewise, the Spirit of God and the Spirit of Jesus can dwell in the body of Jesus. The body is a temple and if one keeps one's temple clean, God's Spirit will guide one when necessary and in difficult times. He can take it over from one. In that instance, the Holy Spirit of God will do the speaking.

The manifestation of God's Spirit was also seen in His holy angels. This doesn't mean that the angel is God, but rather God speaking through His angels.

Exodus 3:2

And *the angel* **of the Lord** appeared unto him in a flame of fire out of the midst of a bush: and he looked, and, behold, the bush burned with fire, and the bush was not consumed.

...Moreover *he said, I am the God* of thy father, the God of Abraham, the God of Isaac, and the God of Jacob. And Moses hid his face; for he was afraid to look upon God.

Conclusion

Within this Biblical context, God's Spirit has manifested Himself in the flesh of His children, not of God Himself being born as a man to take on our sins and to die for them, for God cannot die and cannot take sin.

When His Son was sent to take on our sins, God's Holy Spirit had forsaken him, for God's Spirit is Holy and cannot take sin.

Matthew 27:46

And about the ninth hour Jesus cried with a loud voice, saying, Eli, Eli, lama sabachthani? That is to say, *My God, my God, why hast thou forsaken me?*

Argument 11

Genesis 1:26
And God said, Let **Us** make man in **Our** image, after *Our* likeness.

Does this verse imply that God is plural and that He is triune?
According to the Bible, God consists of seven spirits:
Revelation 4:5
And out of the throne proceeded lightnings and thunderings and voices: and there were seven lamps of fire burning before the throne, which are *the seven Spirits of God*.

These seven spirits are not seven persons but His seven holy attributes. Man is created in the likeness of these attributes, which most probably are the following:
1. The spirit of Justice
2. The spirit of Truth
3. The spirit of Jealousy
4. The spirit of Prophecy
5. The spirit of Life
6. The spirit of Grace
7. The spirit of Wisdom

1. Justice
Isaiah 28:6
For a **spirit of justice** to him who sits in judgment,
And for strength to those who turn back the battle at the gate.

2. Truth
John 14:17
The *Spirit of truth*, whom the world cannot receive, because it neither sees Him nor knows Him; but you know Him, for He dwells with you and will be in you.

3. Jealousy

Numbers 5:14

If the **spirit of jealousy** comes upon him and he becomes jealous of his wife, who has defiled herself.

Exodus 20:5

You shall not bow down to them nor serve them. For I, the Lord your God, am a jealous God, visiting the iniquity of the fathers upon the children to the third and fourth generations of those who hate Me.

(It is important to note that **jealousy is not** equitable with **envy.** Like sorrow and anger, jealousy is a justified negative feeling that is caused by our loved ones.

For example:

a.   A son who ignores his average father, but obeys his rich uncle causes the father to become jealous.

b.   A mother who is unsatisfied with her own average child, but praises the child of another causes the child to become jealous.

The father's jealousy is justified because the son belongs rightfully to the father. The child's jealousy is justified because the mother belongs rightfully to the child.

 Envy is an evil feeling through which one wishes to take or destroy that which is not rightfully his or hers.)

4. Prophecy

Revelation 19:10

And I fell at his feet to worship him. But he said to me, "See that you do not do that! I am your fellow servant, and of your brethren who have the testimony of Jesus. Worship God! For the testimony of Jesus is the **spirit of prophecy**."

5. Life
Romans 8:2
For the law of the **Spirit of life** in Christ Jesus hath made me free
from the law of sin and death.

6.Grace
Zechariah 12:10
And I will pour on the house of David and on the inhabitants of
Jerusalem the **Spirit of grace and supplication**; then they will look
on Me whom they pierced. Yes, they will mourn for Him as one
mourns for his only son, and grieve for Him as one grieves for a
firstborn.

7. Wisdom
Exodus 28:3
O you shall speak to all who are gifted artisans, whom I have filled
with the **spirit of wisdom**, that they may make Aaron's garments, to
consecrate him, that he may minister to Me as priest.

Proverbs 8:12, 22-24
"I, wisdom, dwell with prudence, And find
out knowledge and discretion.
"The Lord possessed me at the beginning of His way, Before
His works of old.
I have been established from everlasting, From the beginning, *before
there was ever an earth.*
When there were no depths I was brought forth, When
there were no fountains abounding with water.

Conclusion

God created man after His different attributes, which are described in the bible as spirits. These attributes of God were with Him in the beginning and form one Person whom we call God.

Only **one Person** with multiple attributes created the world:
Isaiah 44:24
Thus saith the Lord, thy redeemer, and he that formed thee from the womb, I am the Lord that maketh all things; that stretcheth forth the heavens *alone*; that spreadeth abroad the earth *by myself*;

The son of man is made in the image of these seven spirits:
Revelation 5:6
And I beheld, and, lo, in the midst of the throne and of the four beasts, and in the midst of the elders, **stood a Lamb as it had been slain, having seven horns and seven eyes, which are the seven Spirits of God sent forth into all the earth.**

Isaiah 11:2
And the spirit of the Lord shall rest upon him, **the spirit of wisdom and understanding, the spirit of counsel and might, the spirit of knowledge and of the fear of the Lord;**

Argument 12

Revelation 2:8
And unto the angel of the church in Smyrna write; These things saith
the first and the last, which was dead, and is alive;

It is clear that Jesus is the first and the last, but God is also called the
First and the Last or Alpha and Omega. Does this entail that Jesus is
God?

Trinitarians attempt to use all of Jesus' titles to claim that Jesus is
God, but it is always important to begin by looking at the meaning of
each title. The meaning of being first and last is to be unique, rather
than to be God.

For example:
1. This is my first and last cigarette.
2. You are my first and last love.

We are not unique, for all people are born from men, only one man
was begotten by God, this is His Son, named Adam. The Bible clearly
shows that Adam/Jesus are one and the same person who came to
Earth at different times and with different names which served their
purposes in God's plan.
Adam/Jesus is the only begotten son of God, and his title is therefore
the first and the last.

Conclusion

Jesus/Adam is the only (meaning first and last) begotten human son of God.

John 3:18

.... because he hath not believed in the name of **the only** *begotten Son of God.*

God is the only (meaning first and last) God.

Isaiah 44:6

Thus says the Lord, ...

"I am the First and I am the Last; ***Besides Me there is no God.***"

Argument 13

Revelation 19:16
And he hath on his vesture and on his thigh a name written, ***King of Kings,*** And **Lord Of Lords**.

Do Jesus' titles as King of Kings and Lord of Lords imply that he is God?

Trinitarians affirm this, but it is necessary to consult the Bible regarding these titles:
Ezekiel 26:7
For thus saith the Lord God; Behold, I will bring upon Tyrus *Nebuchadrezzar* king of Babylon, ***a king of kings***, from the north, with horses, and with chariots, and with horsemen, and companies, and much people.

From the story of Nebuchadnezzar we can see that God has made this man a king over a group of other kings, and so he was titled by God a king of kings.
The following shows that king Jehoiakim became a servant to king Nebuchadnezzar.
2 Kings 24:1
In his days Nebuchadnezzar king of Babylon came up, and Jehoiakim became his servant three years: then he turned and rebelled against him.

Prophet Daniel said to Nebuchadnezzar:
Daniel 2:37
Thou, O king, art a **king of kings**: for the God of heaven hath given thee a kingdom, power, and strength, and glory.

Conclusion

These Bible verses show that the title "King of Kings" refers to a King over a group of other Kings, from which it does not follow that a person such as Nebuchadnezzar is a god.

There can be many Kings who have power over other Kings. The Messiah is also titled a King over other kings and Lords, but God is God over all the Kings, all the Lords, and all the creatures.

Argument 14

They who deny that Jesus is God are heretics and are not real Christians.

There is no verse in the King James Version of the Bible (KJV) that affirms this claim.

Aggressive Trinitarians intimidate other Christians by claiming that those who do not agree with their doctrine are heretics or anti-Christs, and will probably be cast out to find themselves walking on a narrow road.

Theologian, Physicist and mathematician **Isaac Newton** was a devout Christian, as a free thinker he is an apt example of a christian who was branded as a heretic after he disagreed with the Trinity concept.

Argument 15

God is the only Rock.
Psalm 18:31
For who is God save the LORD? Or who is **a rock** save our God?

Jesus is also a Rock.
1 Corinthians 10:4
And did all drink the same spiritual drink: for they drank of that spiritual Rock that followed them: and that **Rock was Christ**.

Trinitarians argue that there can only be one Rock and that this title always refers to God. Since Jesus is called "the Rock" in Paul's letters, they assume that Jesus is God.

However, "rock" is not an equivalent term for God, but rather a figurative word with which to refer to a particular type of foundation. In Psalm 18:31 during the times of the Old Covenant, the only rock that was known to king David was God. In the New Covenant, God sent His son to be a 'rock' for His people, when Jesus left he made Peter a 'rock' for the gentiles to build his church.
Matthew 16:18
And I say also unto thee, That thou art **Peter**, and upon **this rock** I will build my church; and the gates of hell shall not prevail against it.

Conclusion

Rock figural means being a foundation, not being a god.

Argument 16

1 John 5:8
For there are **three** that bear witness in heaven: *the Father, the word, and the Holy Spirit; and these three are one.*

Trinitarians suggest that there are three 'persons' in Heaven who witness, and that these three persons are one: the heavenly Father, Jesus as the Word, and the Holy Spirit.
It is important to consider the context of the chapter containing John's letter:
1 John 5:8
For there are three that bear witness in heaven: the Father, the word, and the Holy Spirit; and these three are one
If we receive the witness of men, the witness of God is greater; *for this is the witness of God which He has testified of His Son.*

This chapter describes three ways in which God testifies that Jesus is His Son:
1. As the Father.
2. In His Word (prophecies).
3. By His Holy Spirit.

These three forms of testimony are not three separate persons. They came from one God who testified as a Father, through the prophets (words), and through a confirmation with His Spirit (in the form of a dove).

1. God as Father testified that Jesus is His son:
Matthew 3:17
And suddenly a voice came from heaven, saying, "This is My beloved Son, in whom I am well pleased."

2. Prophets who received the word testified that Jesus is God's son:
Luke 3:2
Annas and Caiaphas being the high priests, *the word of God came unto John* the son of Zacharias in the wilderness.

John 1:34
And I have seen and testified that this is the Son of God.

3. God's Spirit confirmed that Jesus is the son of God:
Matthew 3:16
When He had been baptized, Jesus came up immediately from the water; and behold, the heavens were opened to Him, and He saw the *Spirit of God* descending like a dove and alighting upon Him.

The Father, the word (prophecies), and the Holy Spirit are the three that are from one Person and bore witness to Jesus being His Son. Jesus cannot be part of these three, for he said:
John 5:31
If I bear witness of Myself, My witness is not true. There is another who bears witness of Me, and I know that the witness which He witnesses of Me is true.
You have sent to John, and he has borne witness to the truth. And the Father Himself, who sent Me, has testified of Me.

The Word in 1 John 5:9 stands for the prophecies. In certain passages, the prophets of the Bible, such as John the Baptist, do not speak their own words, but rather pass on the word of God. This word is not a person, but rather a prophecy, commandment, or other message from God.

The following passage is one of many examples:

Ezekiel 6:3

And say, Ye mountains of Israel, hear *the word* of the Lord God;
Thus saith the Lord God to the mountains, and to the hills, to the
rivers, and to the valleys; Behold, I, even I, will bring a sword upon
you, and I will destroy your high places.

Conclusion

God bore witness of Jesus as a Father, through His Words and by His
Spirit and these three are indeed one Person.

Argument 17

Hebrews 1:8
But to **the Son He says**: "Your throne, **O God**, is forever and ever."

This verse clearly shows that the Son is called God. However, the problem with the book of Hebrews is that it is unclear who wrote it. Hebrews is actually an apocryphal book, because we do not know who its author is. Some suggest that Paul the Evangelist is the author, but the style of Hebrews differs significantly from the style of the undisputed letters of Paul. In addition, the author of Hebrews was part of the second generation of Christians, while Paul considered himself to be part of the first generation of Christians.

The author of Hebrews:
Hebrews 2:3
How shall we escape if we neglect so great a salvation, which at the first began to be spoken by the Lord, and was confirmed *to us by those **who heard Him.***

Paul:
Galatians 1:12
For I neither received it from man, nor was I taught it, but it came through the revelation of Jesus Christ.

The author of Hebrews gave the impression that the angels are not sons of God, thereby contradicting the other Biblical books, which describe the angels as the sons of God.

Angels not as sons of God:
Hebrews 1:5
For to which of the angels did He ever say: "**You are My Son**, today I have begotten You."

This is contradicted in:

Genesis 6:2

That **the sons of God** saw the daughters of men.

Job 1:6

Now there was a day when **the sons of God** came to present themselves before the Lord, and Satan also came among them.

It is of great importance to know the source of any writings, for the apostles warned that already in their time, many false Christians were active:

2 Corinthians 11:13

For such are **false apostles,** deceitful workers, transforming themselves into the apostles of Christ.

Revelation 2:2

I know thy works, and thy labour, and thy patience, and how thou canst not bear them which are evil: and thou hast tried them which **say they are apostles, and are not**, and hast found them liars.

1 John 2:19

They went out from us, but they were not of us; for if they had been of us, they would have continued with us; but they went out that they might be made manifest, that none of them were of us.

Conclusion

The book of Hebrews is an apocryphal book, and needless for knowing and understanding the Gospel.

Argument 18

Zechariah 12:10
And I will pour on the house of David and on the inhabitants of Jerusalem the Spirit of grace and supplication; *then they will look on Me whom they pierced*. Yes, they will mourn for him as one mourns for his only son, and grieve for Him as one grieves for a firstborn.

This verse clearly shows that God will be pierced, but that another one will be mourned. This verse seems illogical in stating that they will mourn over "him" when they have pierced "Me". It is important to bear in mind that translation errors are possible and have occurred, including some instances in the KJV.

Another example of a translation error in the KJV:

KJV from 1631:
Omitting an important "not" from Exodus 20:14, the seventh commandment states: "Thou shalt commit adultery." The printers were fined and the few surviving copies that still exist today are known as "the Wicked Bible".

To verify whether the KJV of Zechariah 12:10 is correct and as the book of Zechariah is an O.T. book, it is necessary to consult the Masoretic Text (the authoritative Hebrew text of the Tanakh/O.T.). The Jewish Publication Society (JPS) offers the correct English translation of Zechariah 12:10.

JPS Tanakh:
Zechariah 12:10
And I will pour upon the house of David,
And upon the inhabitants of Jerusalem,
The spirit of grace and of supplication; And they shall **look unto Me because they have** *thrust him through;*

And they shall mourn for him, as one mourneth for his only son, And shall be in bitterness for him, as one that is in bitterness for his first-born.

Conclusion

Translated from the more reliable Masoretic Text and contrary to the KJV translation, this verse clearly states that they will look upon "Me" because they have pierced "him", and that they will also mourn for "him". The translation from the Masoretic Text is logical, clear, and in agreement with the other scriptures.

Argument 19

Isaiah 6:1
In the year that king Uzziah died I saw also the Lord sitting upon a
throne, high and lifted up, and his train filled the temple.

John 12:41
These things said Esaias, when he saw his glory, and spake of him.

**Isaiah saw Jesus sitting in the Fathers throne, therefore Trinitarians
assume that Jesus is God.**
However the scripture clearly explains that God shares His throne
with His Son, and eventually also with the offspring of His Son.
Revelation 3:21
To him that overcometh will I grant *to sit* with me *in my throne, even
as I also overcame,* **and am** *set down* **with my Father** *in his throne.*

Conclusion

Sincere Christians will also sit on the throne with Jesus and God as
one family. While God shares His throne with us, this does not entail
that He shares His glory of being a God with us.

Argument 20

2peter:1:20
Who verily was foreordained **before the foundation of the world,**
but was manifest in these last times for you,

Jesus was with God in the beginning before the world began.

Trinitarians claim that Jesus existed before planet earth was created
In the bible there is a **difference between the World and the Earth;**

When the scripture refers to the planet it's called earth :

Genesis 1:1
In the beginning God created the heaven and the **earth.**

Psalm 24:1
The **earth** is the Lord's, and the fulness thereof; the world, and they
that dwell therein.

Matthew 5:18
For verily I say unto you, Till heaven and **earth** pass, one jot or one
tittle shall in no wise pass from the law, till all be fulfilled.

When the scripture refers to human society it's called the world :

John 15:19
If ye were of the world, **the world would love** his own: but because
ye are not of the world, but I have chosen you out of the world,
therefore the world hateth you.

Luke 2:1
And it came to pass in those days, that there went out a decree from
Caesar Augustus that all **the world should be taxed**.

Prophets were present since the world began
Luke 1:70
As he spake by the mouth of his **holy prophets, which have been since the world began.**

Prophets were killed from the foundation of the world
Luke 11:50
That the **blood of all the prophets, which was shed from the foundation of the world,** may be required of this generation;

The Father loved His son before the foundation of the world
John 17:24
Father, I will that they also, whom thou hast given me, be with me where I am; that they may behold my glory, which thou hast given me: **for thou lovedst me before the foundation of the world.**

Conclusion

In many cases the foundation of the world clearly represents the beginning of the human society, the only man that lived before the foundations of the 'world' was Adam.

Argument 21

Matthew 9:2
And, behold, they brought to him a man sick of the palsy, lying on a bed: and Jesus seeing their faith said unto the sick of the palsy; Son, be of good cheer; thy sins be forgiven thee. 3 And, behold, certain of the scribes said within themselves, This man blasphemeth.

Jesus forgave sins.

Trinitarians believe just like the jewish scribes that only can God forgive sins.
Lets look at what Jesus said:

John 20:22
And when he had said this, he breathed on them, and saith unto them, Receive ye the Holy Ghost: 23 **whose soever sins ye remit**, they are remitted unto them; and whose soever sins ye retain, they are retained.

Matthew 18:21
Then came Peter to him, and said, Lord, how oft shall **my brother sin against me, and I forgive him**? till seven times? Jesus saith unto him, I say not unto thee, Until seven times: but, Until seventy times seven.

Conclusion

According to scripture every man is capable of forgiving sin.

Conclusion about the Trinity

The trinity doctrine is not unique and commonly teached in many pagan sources, but it has no foundation in the Gospel of the Bible. Trinitarians who attempt to claim that the Trinity is also in the Bible are failing by lack of understanding, because common sense and the general message of the Bible will be against them.

With their complex and not to comprehend gospel they partially misrepresent Christianity which made many people confused causing the rise of religions like Islam, Jehovah Witnesses, Mormonism etc. The real truth is that Christianity from the Bible is a simple, clear and easy to understand message.

We can sum-up the main differences between God and Jesus:

God is Spirit.
John 24:4
God is **a Spirit**: and they that worship him must worship him in spirit and in truth.

Jesus is not a spirit.
Luke 24:39
Behold my hands and my feet, that it is I myself: handle me, and see; for **a spirit hath not flesh and bones**, as ye see me have.

Jesus is a man.

Acts 17:31 because He has appointed a day on which He will judge the world in righteousness by *that man* whom He has ordained. He has given assurance of this to all by raising him from the dead."

God is not a man
Hosea 11:9
I will not execute the fierceness of My anger; I will not again destroy Ephraim.
For I am God, **and *not man*,** The Holy One in your midst; And I will not come with terror

Jesus has a God
John 20:17
Jesus said to her, "Do not cling to Me, for I have not yet ascended to My Father; but go to My brethren and say to them, 'I am ascending to **My Father and your Father,** and to *My God* and your God.'"

God has no god
1 Kings 8:23
And he said, LORD God of Israel**, there is no God like thee**, in heaven above, or on earth beneath, who keepest covenant and mercy with thy servants that walk before thee with all their heart

God allowed Jesus to be tempted.
Matt 4:2
And he was there in the wilderness forty days, **tempted of Satan**; and was with the wild beasts; and the angels ministered unto him.

God cannot be tempted.
James 1:13
Let no man say when he is tempted, I am tempted of God: for *God cannot be tempted* **with evil**, neither tempteth he any man:

The nature of God

God is singular in person
Isaiah 46:9
Remember the former things of old: for **I** am God, and there is none
else; **I** am God, and there is none like **ME**,

Deuteronomy 6:4
Hear, O Israel: The Lord our God is **one Lord**

God is plural in spirits

Genesis 1:26
And God said, **Let US** make man in **OUR** image, after **OUR** likeness:
and let them have dominion over the fish of the sea, and over the fowl
of the air, and over the cattle, and over all the earth, and over every
creeping thing that creepeth upon the earth..

Revelation 4:5
And out of the throne proceeded lightnings and thunderings and
voices: and there were seven lamps of fire burning before the throne,
which are **the seven Spirits of God.**

Revelation 5:6
And I beheld, and, lo, in the midst of the throne and of the four beasts,
and in the midst of the elders, stood a Lamb as it had been slain,
having seven horns and seven eyes, which are the **seven Spirits of
God sent forth into all the earth.**

God is the Creator
Isaiah 40:28
Hast thou not known? hast thou not heard, that the everlasting God,
the Lord**, the Creator of the ends of the earth,** fainteth not, neither is
weary? there is no searching of his understanding.

Roman 1:25
Who changed the truth of God into a lie, and worshipped and served the creature more than **the Creator**, who is blessed for ever. Amen.

No other gods
Deuteronomy 32:39
See now that I, even I, am he, and **there is no god with me**: I kill, and I make alive; I wound, and I heal: neither is there any that can deliver out of my hand.

Are there other gods?

Exodus 23:32
Thou shalt make no covenant with them, nor with **their gods**

These 'other gods' are described as idols or false gods.
Isaiah 42:17
They shall be turned back, they shall be greatly ashamed, that trust in graven images, that say to the molten images, **Ye are our gods.**

Psalm 96:5
For **all the gods of the nations are idols:** but the Lord made the heavens.

God said there are no other living gods
Isaiah 43:10
Ye are my witnesses, saith the Lord, and my servant whom I have chosen: that ye may know and believe me, and understand that I am he: **before me there was no God formed, neither shall there be after me.**

The nature of Jesus

Four biblical testimonies about Jesus that are undeniable.

Jesus is a man
1 Timothy 2:5
For there is one God, and one mediator **between God and men, the man Christ Jesus**;

1.God about Jesus:
Matthew 3:17
"This is *My beloved son*, with whom I am well pleased."

2.Prophet John about Jesus:
John 1:34
I have seen and testified that this is *the Son of* **God**."

3.The disciples about Jesus:
John 20:31
that ye might **believe that Jesus is** the Christ, *the Son of* **God**; and that believing ye might have life through his name.

Jesus developes in wisdom
Luke 2:52
52 And Jesus increased in wisdom and stature, and in favour with God and men

Given all these verses there is no question that we can call Jesus the son of God.
It would be very wrong to ignore these very clear statements and make and spread one's own assumptions.

Jesus compared with Adam

Jesus pre-existed

After examining the verses in their entirety we can say for sure that there is no biblical foundation for the Trinity doctrine, but we have seen in that Jesus existed even before Abraham was born.

John 8:57
Then said the Jews unto him, Thou art not yet fifty years old, and hast thou seen Abraham?
58 Jesus said unto them, Verily, verily, I say unto you, **Before Abraham was, I am.**

And he was already created before the world's foundation.

1Peter 1:20
Who verily was foreordained before **the foundation of the world,** but was manifest in these last times for you,

John 17:5
And now, O Father, glorify thou me with thine own self **with the glory which I had with thee before the world was.**

(to be clear: glory means honor)

Let us look what the link is between Adam the Man of sorrows and Jesus also called the Man of sorrows.

The Bible clearly states that Jesus is the begotten Son of God Jesus is in fact the ONLY begotten Son of God, but Adam is also the only begotten son of God:

(To be clear:"to beget" means to produce or create or to be a direct father of)

The genealogy shows that every man was begotten by another man except for the first man Adam.

Luke 3:38

..which was the son of Enos, which was the son of Seth, which was the son of *Adam, which was the son of God.*

What is son of Man

Luke 9:22

Saying, *The Son of Man* must suffer many things, and be rejected of the elders and chief priests and scribes, and be slain, and be raised the third day.

According to the genealogy Adam is the only begotten son of God, but the angels are also the numerous begotten(direct) sons of God:

Job 1:6

Now there was a day when **the sons of God** came to present themselves before the Lord, and Satan came also among them.

We know from Job 1:6 and Luke 3:38 that God has two types of begotten sons:
1. the first and last begotten human son. (Adam/Jesus)
2. the many begotten cherubs or better known as angelical sons.

Jesus refers to himself as to be the son of man.

here are two possibilities:
1 Jesus was the son of *a* man
2 Jesus was the son **made of** Man

In the beginning God created many cherub sons but only one human son.

79

Jesus made it clear on which type of son he is by referring to be the son of Man which stands for the son made of Man.

For example:
>a cup of gold or a table of wood tells us of which material the product is made, likewise by saying the son of Man tells of which nature this son was made.

Many people assume that the son of Man means to be the son of a man, but its seems that Jesus never considered himself to be the son of a human, because of the way he addressed his 'mother'.
If Jesus is the reincarnation of Adam, then he would not see Mary as his mother.

Matt 12:47
Then one said unto him, Behold, **thy mother** and thy brethren stand without, desiring to speak with thee. But he answered and said unto him that told him, *Who is my mother*? and who are my brethren?

John 2:3
And when they wanted wine, the mother of Jesus saith unto him, They have no wine. Jesus saith unto her, *Woman, what have I to do with thee?* mine hour is not yet come.

Note: There are people in the Bible who are called **like** the son of God (indirect) or are to become a child of God (indirect), this is not the same as being the begotten (direct born) son of God.
For example, a grandfather can call his grandchild "son", but he is not his begotten son.

The Connection between Adam and Jesus

Its clear that Jesus pre-existed, with the Bible we can easily trace back who Jesus was.
To do this we have to go to the book of Genesis to the part that describes the beginning of everything.
We simply have to look for a man that was begotten by God, was given glory by God and was created before the foundation of our world.

1.Glory with God:

- The First man Adam is given dominion over God's creation:
  Genesis 1:28
  Then God blessed them, and God said to them, "Be fruitful and multiply; fill the earth and subdue it; *have dominion* over the fish of the sea, over the birds of the air, and **over every living thing that moves on the earth.**"

- Jesus dominion over creation wil be restored:
  John 17:5
  And now, O Father, glorify you me with your own self with the glory *which I had with you* **before** the **world** was.

  Revelation 11:14
  And the seventh angel sounded; and there were great voices in heaven, saying, The kingdoms of this world are become the kingdoms of our Lord, and of his Christ; and he shall reign for ever and ever.

The Image of God
- Adam is begotten by God and is also the image of God
  Genesis 1:27
  So God created man in his own image, in the image of God created He *him*; male and female created he them.

Adam became equal with God in knowing good and evil.
And the Lord God said, "Behold, *the man has become as
one of Us*, **to know good and evil**. And now, lest he put forth
his hand and take also of the tree of life, and eat and live
forever"

- Jesus is the image of God and also became equal with God:
  Philippians 2:6
  Who, being in the **form of God**, thought it not robbery
  to be **equal with God**

The Son of God was created in the beginning
- Jesus was created before the foundation of the world.
  1Peter 1:20
  Who verily was foreordained before **the foundation** of the
  world, but was manifest in these last times for you,

- Adam is clearly created before the foundation of the human
  world, but he was also created before the foundation of the
  earth was finished on the seventh day:
  Genesis 1:27,31
  So God created man in his own image, in the image of God
  created he him; male and female created he them.
  And God saw everything that he had made, and, behold, it
  was very good. And the evening and the morning *were the
  sixth day.*

God finished the heavens and the earth after seven days.
Genesis 2:1
Thus the heavens and the earth were finished, and all the host of
them. *And on the seventh day God ended his work* which he had
made; and he rested on the seventh day from all his work which he
had made. And God blessed the seventh day, and sanctified it:
because that in it he had rested from all his work which God created
and made. These are the generations of the heavens and of the earth

when they were created, in the day that the Lord God made the earth and the heavens,

God said that Man (Gods Image) is vital for the foundation of the earth.

Earths water cycle (rain) wouldn't start, without Adam.
Genesis 2:5
And every plant of the field before it was in the earth, and every herb of the field before it grew: for the Lord *God **had not caused it to rain upon the earth**,* and there was not a Man to till the ground.

Notice that one of Earths critical foundations the rain started after Adam was created.

Genesis clearly describes that Adam was formed before the foundation of the world, and he was with God and was given dominion over paradise.

Adam the root of David
According to the genealogy Adam is the root of David and Jesus is the offspring of David, but when we read carefully, we see that Jesus also said that he is not only the offspring, but also the Root of David:

Revelation 22:16
I Jesus have sent mine angel to testify unto you these things in the churches. *I am the root* **and the offspring of David**, and the bright and morning star.

We can see clearly in the genealogy of Luke 3:23 that the root of David is Adam and the offspring of David is Jesus. The root (Adam) and the offspring (Jesus) are both called the son of God and Jesus said he is both.
Genealogy:
Luke 3:23 - 38

And **Jesus** (offspring) himself began to be about thirty years of age, being the son of Joseph, which was the son of Heli, Which was the son of Matthat, ..., which was the son of David, which was the son of Jesse, which was the son of Seth which was the son of **Adam** (root), which was the son of God.

Therefore, Jesus; the son of God is an offspring of David, and David came from the root Adam, who is also the son of God.
Those who want to suggest that the root is God Himself, according to Jesus the root and the offspring are both son of God.

The offspring of Jesus.

The Bible states that Jesus would come and save his own offspring. Jesus would see his offspring:
Isaiah 53:10
Yet it pleased the Lord to bruise him; he hath put him to grief: when thou shalt make his soul an offering for sin, *he shall see his seed*, he shall prolong his days, and the pleasure of the Lord shall prosper in his hand.

By Adam all living are begotten:
Genesis 3:20
And Adam called his wife's name Eve, because she was the **mother of all living.**

By Jesus all living were begotten
1 Corinthians 8:6
But to us there is but one God, the Father, of whom are all things, and we in him; and one Lord Jesus Christ, *by* whom are all things, and *we by him.*

Jesus who was around thirty years old, addressed people as his children.
Matthew 9:22
But Jesus turned around, and when He saw her He said, "Be of good cheer, *daughter*; your faith has made you well." And the woman was made well from that hour.

Jesus gave parables that suggest the people being his offspring.
John 15:5
"I am the *vine*, you are the *branches*.

Matthew 9:2
And, behold, they brought to him a man sick of the palsy, lying on a bed: and Jesus seeing their faith said unto the sick of the palsy; **Son,** be of good cheer; thy sins be forgiven thee.

According to the Bible, there are two persons who are father to all mankind: the first man Adam and ofcourse God who is the Father of Adam.

It is just and logic that God would send Adam to free, save and bare the judgement for his own offspring.
This also clarifies why Jesus in his life never got married, since all people with the exception of Eve must have been his children.

Was Adam a sinner

Many churches put Adam in a negative light, because they accuse Adam of sin and also assign to him the blame for our fall.
If Adam really desired to sin against God then it is very strange that God, who is the most righteous Judge, would bestow compassion upon Adam and his offspring, but curses the Serpent and his offspring and even instructs their annihilation.

When we read carefully, the implication that Adam sinned is not in agreement with the trial that started in Genesis.

What Trinitarians should realize is that Adam was sinless. Before eating from the tree of Good and Evil, he and his wife had no knowledge of Evil, so they were not capable of committing sin.

When God looked at Adam and Eve, He said:

Genesis 1:31

Then God saw everything that He had made, and indeed it was **very good.** So the evening and the morning were the sixth day.

The trial and judgement in Genesis 3.

After the first command was being broken, God asked Adam why he ate from the tree, and Adam truthfully replied;.

Genesis 3:12

Then the man said, "The woman whom You gave to be with me, *she gave me of the tree*, and I ate."

It's logical that Adam who had no knowledge of Evil had no reason to suspect the wife he was given by God.

God confronted the woman and she truthfully explained that she was deceived by the Serpent.

Genesis 3:13

And the Lord God said unto the woman, What is this that thou hast done? And the woman said, The serpent *deceived* **me**, and I did eat.

Eve like Adam had no knowledge of Evil, meaning she couldn't recognize deceit and therefor had no reason to suspect the Serpent. After eating she gained the knowledge to know that she was deceived and used by the Serpent to give Adam to eat from the forbidden tree. This Satan who used this deception was the true sinner and was justly punished for his sin.

Genesis 3:14

So the Lord God said to the serpent:

"Because you have done this, *You are cursed* **more** than all cattle, And more than every beast of the field;
On your belly you shall go, And you shall eat dust **all the days of your life.**

Revelation 12 :9
So the great dragon was cast out, *that serpent* **of old,** *called the Devil and Satan,* *who deceives* the whole world; he was cast to the earth, and his angels were cast out with him.

After the deception of Satan, the knowledge of Evil entered the human race through Adam.
Genesis 3:22
And the LORD God said, Behold, the man is become as one of us, to know good and evil: and now, lest he put forth his hand, and take also of the tree of life, and eat, and live for ever.

Having knowledge of Evil is not a sin, for even God knows what evil is.
Genesis 3:22
Then the Lord God said, "Behold, the man has become like one of Us, **to know good** *and evil.*

But to make use of this knowledge is a sin. The first human who made use of this knowledge was Cain, by committing murder.
Genesis 4:8
And Cain talked with Abel his brother: and it came to pass, when they were in the field, that Cain rose up against Abel his brother, *and slew him.*

Adam a transgressor
Paul in the beginning of his conversion mentioned in one of his first letters that Adam had transgressed.
Romans 5:14

Nevertheless death reigned from Adam to Moses, even over them that had not sinned after the similitude of *Adam's transgression*, who is the figure of him that was to come.

The apostle Paul was a sincere truth-seeker, however this does not entail that he from his birth was fully developed in understanding the scripture.
The apostles had their disagreements and debates about understanding the scripture.
Here is an letter of Paul wherein he describes his disagreement with the apostle Peter:
Galatians 2:11
Now **when *Peter* had come** to Antioch, *I withstood him to his face, because he was to be blamed*;   for before certain men came from James, he would eat with the Gentiles; but when they came, he withdrew and separated himself, fearing those who were of the circumcision. And the rest of the Jews also played the hypocrite with him, so that even Barnabas was carried away with *their hypocrisy*

In one of Paul's final and last letters, his view of Adam is amended, and he wrote:
1 Timothy 2:14
And Adam was not deceived, *but the woman being deceived, fell into transgression.*

What about the first father that sinned ?
The book of Isaiah describes that a first father had sinned;
Isaiah 43:27
Thy first father hath sinned, and thy teachers have transgressed
against me.

The Bible describes that every nation has a first father.
The first father of Eber:
Genesis 10:21
Unto Shem also, **the father of all the children of Eber**, the brother
of Japheth the elder, even to him were children born.

The first father of Canaan:
Genesis 9:22
And Ham, **the father of Canaan**, saw the nakedness of his father,
and told his two brethren without.

The first father of Israel:
Genesis 35:10
And God said unto him, Thy name is Jacob: thy name shall not be
called any more **Jacob, but Israel shall be thy name**: and he called
his name Israel.

Genesis 49:2
Gather yourselves together, and hear, ye sons of Jacob; and hearken
unto **Israel your father**.

So who is the first father described in Isaiah 43?
There are two options here:
1. The first father of all the nations, which is Adam.
2. The first father of only the nation of Israel, which is Jacob.

Again context is very important to decide in this issue.
Let us first look at who the chapter is addressed to:
Isaiah 43:1
But now thus saith the Lord that created thee, *O Jacob*, and he that
formed thee, *O Israel*, Fear not: for I have redeemed thee, I have
called thee by thy name; thou art mine.

The chapter is clearly only addressed to the nation of Jacob/Israel.
Let us now look at the outcome of this first father that sinned
Isaiah 43:27-28
Thy first father hath sinned, and thy teachers have transgressed
against me.
Therefore I have profaned the princes of the sanctuary, *and have
given Jacob to the curse, and Israel to reproaches.*

Because of the sin of the first father of Israel, Jacob was given to the
curse and his nation Israel to reproach.
If this chapter was about Adam than not only Israel but all the nations
of the world would be addressed in this chapter.
From the entirety of this chapter one can strongly conclude that Jacob
is the one addressed as the first father of Israel rather than Adam.

Reincarnation

Is it possible that God would send Adam with a new name to save us from sin? Is this how God works?
The Bible clearly tells us that God is able to send a person back to earth.
He has demonstrated this by sending the prophet John as the reincarnation of the prophet Elijah.
God gave Elijah his new name, John, when he became born again.

Maleachi 4:5
Behold, **I will send you Elijah** the prophet before the coming of the great and dreadful day of the Lord:

Matt 17:11
But I say to you that *Elijah has come already*, and they did not know him but did to him whatever they wished. Likewise the Son of Man is also about to suffer at their hands." Then the disciples understood that He spoke to them of *John the Baptist*.

Likewise, God gave Adam a new name when he was born again as Jesus, which means Saviour of his people.
When the Son of God comes on the Last Day, he will write this new name upon his followers.
Revelation 3: 12
He who overcomes, I will make him a pillar in the temple of My God, and he shall go out no more. I will write on him the name of My God and the name of the city of My God, the New Jerusalem, which comes down out of heaven from My God. And I will write on him *My new name.*

If Jesus is the new name, then what was the old name?
Jesus also said that he was leaving the world again.
John 16:28

I came forth from the Father, and am come into the world: *again*, **I leave the world,** and go to the Father.

This type of reincarnation should not be confused with the reincarnation concept of Hinduism which teaches that reincarnation is a standard continuous process that involves all animals, plants, bugs and humans.

Adam, Melchizedeck & Jesus

What about Melchizedeck from where did this very essential priest came and where did he go?
Genesis 14:18
And **Melchizedek** *king of Salem* brought forth **bread and wine**: and he was *the priest of the most high God.*
And he blessed him, and said, Blessed be Abram of the most high God, possessor of heaven and earth

One could easily recognizes who Melchizedeck is, this was the figure of a King that was also the High Priest who met Abraham with bread and wine.
In the New Testament Jesus is the king and high priest who comes with bread and wine.

Melchizedeck or Malki Zedeck King of Salem was not an earthly king and Salem (Peace) was not a city.
Malki Zedeck King of Salem is not a name but a title which means; King of Righteousness and King of Peace. And according to Jesus he was the one who met with Abraham and Abraham was rejoiced.
John 8:48
Your father Abraham rejoiced to see my day, *and he saw it and was glad."*
Then the Jews said to Him, "You are not yet fifty years old, and have *You seen Abraham?"*
Jesus said to them, "Most assuredly, I say to you, **before Abraham was, I am."**

As the High Priest of God, he came to bless Abraham and after his blessing the priesthood was given to the descendants of Abraham.

King David saw in his vision how God said unto Jesus the king of Righteousness (malki-zedeck):

Psalm 110:4

The Lord said *unto my Lord,* Sit thou at my right hand, until I make thine enemies thy footstool.

The Lord shall send the rod of thy strength out of Zion: rule thou in the midst of thine enemies.

Thy people shall be willing in the day of thy power, in the beauties of holiness from the womb of the morning: thou hast the dew of thy youth

The Lord hath sworn, and will not repent, *Thou art a priest for ever after the order of Melchizedek.* (King of Righteousness)

When the time of the Levitical priest was completed then this King of Righteousness and of Peace returned to take back the priesthood and fulfil the final atonement for sin.

Leviticus 4:20

So the priest shall make atonement for them, and it shall be forgiven them.

Conclusion about Adam being Jesus

There is only one begotten Man by God, he received different names
in different times serving their purposes.
1 he was created as Adam meaning first Man.
2 he came again as Malki-Zedeck to bless Abraham.
3 he came back again to complete the final priestly duties for our
   salvation with a new name; Jesus meaning Saviour.

Since the earthly man became a heavenly man, so shall his earthly
children become heavenly children.

Paul wrote to the Corinthians:
1 Corinthians 15:45
And so it is written, "*The first man Adam* became a living being.*"
The last Adam became a life-giving spirit.
As was the man of dust, so also are those who are made of dust; and
as is the heavenly Man, so also are those who are heavenly. And as
**we have borne the image of the man of dust, we shall also bear
the image of the heavenly Man.**

Adam came to earth to bless Abraham and passed on him the priestly
duties.
When Abrahams offspring established the nation of Israel, Adam
returned with a new name to make the final atonement for all nations.
Genesis 28:14
..and in thee and in thy seed shall all the families of the earth be
blessed.

Malachi 1:11
For from the rising of the sun even unto the going down of the same
my name shall be great among the Gentiles; and in every place
incense shall be offered unto my name, and a pure offering:
 When Jesus became baptized and received everlasting life so his
children who choose to be baptized will receive everlasting life.

Matt 3:13
Then cometh Jesus from Galilee to Jordan unto John, to be baptized.

In the end all things shall be made subject under God.
1 Corinthians 15:28
And when all things shall be subdued unto him, then s**hall the Son also himself be subject unto Him that put all things under him,** that God may be all in all.

Hopefully after reading this book Trinitarians will come to realize that their doctrine is a confused illogic mystery that doesn't fit the understandable biblical story about God's nature and the connection with His son Jesus Christ.

Psalm 14:2

The Lord looked down from heaven upon the children of men, to see if there were any that did <u>*understand, and seek God.*</u>

Proverbs 4:7

Wisdom is the principal thing; therefore get wisdom: and with all thy getting <u>*get understanding*</u>*"*

Questions Trinitarians should answer (with answers from the Bible of course)

There are many sayings from Jesus that should wake up anyone who wants to believe that Jesus is God.

Trinitarians often answer questions about the trinity with their own logic, it would be better to seek for the answer in the scripture.

Did Jesus had a God (creator)

Ephesians 1:3

 Blessed be the God and Father of our Lord Jesus Christ, who hath blessed us with all spiritual blessings in heavenly places in Christ:

Will God pray to God?

John 17:15

I(Jesus) pray not that thou shouldest take them out of the world, but that thou shouldest keep them from the evil.

Is God's will separate from God's will?

Matthew 26:39

O my Father, if it be possible, *let this cup pass from me*: nevertheless *not as I (Jesus) will, but as thou wilt.*

Was God sent by God ?

John 5:30

I can of mine own self do nothing: as I hear, I judge: and my judgment is just; because I seek not mine own will, but the will of *the Father which hath sent me(Jesus).*

Did the self-existent God gives life to God?

John 5:26

For as *the Father* has life in Himself, so hath he *given* to the Son to have life in himself

Did Jesus emphasize not to be called good?
Luke 18:19
And Jesus said unto him, Why callest thou me good? none is good, save one, that is, God.

Did Jesus made a declaration to show that he and the Father aren't co equal?
John 14:28
The Father *is greater* than I.

Did God forsake the suffering God?
Matthew 27:46
My God, My God, why hast thou forsaken me (Jesus)?

Did God gave a revelation to God?
Revelation 1:1
The Revelation of Jesus Christ, which *God gave unto him(Jesus)*

Did God ascend to his God?
John 20:17
Jesus saith unto her, Touch me not; for I am not yet ascended to my Father: but go to my brethren, and say unto them, I (Jesus) ascend unto my Father, and your Father; and to my God, and your God.